Images of Yesterday

by Art Gore

AMERICAN WEST PUBLISHING COMPANY

PALO ALTO, CALIFORNIA

LIBRARY OF CONGRESS CATALOGING IN PUBLICATION DATA

Gore, Art, 1926–
    Images of yesterday.

    1. Gore, Art, 1926–   2. Photographers—
Correspondence, reminiscences, etc.   3. Country life—
United States.   I. Title.

TR140.G65A32   779'.92'4   75-6322
ISBN 0-910118-67-1

I often think that Solomon would have been the wiser had he known my father. This kindly man was a country lawyer in the farming town of Raeford, North Carolina, and how he managed to hold us together in those depression and post-depression days is more than I shall ever understand.

I've heard him relate many times how he suffered as a boy on a small farm in the sandy lowlands of North Carolina. Yet somehow he managed to scrounge an education, becoming an honor student at Columbia Law School and winning the gold medal, which he later wore as a watch fob. One day, as I was skipping along beside him while he walked to his one-room law office above the bank, I asked him for a nickel to buy a candy bar. He looked wistfully down at me, turned a pocket inside out, and replied, "Son, I don't even have a nickel."

His clients were always bringing us fatback, sweet potatoes, firewood, and other necessities in exchange for his legal work. Despite the hard times there were some things we always had around our big frame house three blocks from Main Street: onions, popcorn, collard greens, turnips, salt pork—and a variety of cats.

I suppose my father was the one who convinced me there was an all-powerful Being, a Creator of our planet and the universe. Sometimes he would make popcorn for the six of us—

I had four sisters and a brother—and every time we'd get a lecture about popcorn. A miracle, he called it, one that only a Creator could devise—an ingenious little hard seed that exploded inside out into something edible. His logic convinced us all that God had spent at least an hour working out this miracle just for us.

But my father was a far better philosopher than cook. Those evenings when he decided to take over the kitchen, there would be some of the most gosh-awful concoctions one could imagine. He'd call it "pot-licker." Usually it was collard greens boiled with salt pork and sliced onions, with a little vinegar thrown in. He used onions in everything and could give us a dozen reasons why the world would be worse off if God hadn't made them. We learned early to make sandwiches with those big sweet onions you can't buy any more.

I guess my father was in dire financial trouble when my mother died, ten days after I was born (I was premature, weighing less than three pounds, and wasn't supposed to survive). He was just beginning law practice and had to take my older sister and me to live with three old-maid aunts in Fayetteville, twenty miles from Raeford. We remained with them for three years.

Those dear ladies also helped shape my life. They lived

on the outskirts of town in a Victorian home built just after the Civil War. They loved flowers, and on a lot about a half-block long adjacent to the house, they grew beautiful roses and iris that stood taller than my head. These flowers adorned both sides of the altar at the church—my aunts were dyed-in-the-wool Scotch Presbyterians. When I was older and visited them during the summer or on winter weekends, I never escaped church or Sunday school. Nobody but the McArthurs and their relatives sat in the "McArthur pew." There was a silent understanding, among the church members that, since these ladies were the most generous financial sponsors of the church, their pew would remain empty unless they were there to occupy it.

Aunt Maggie was my favorite great-aunt, and her dream was for me to become a minister. It must have perplexed her greatly that I squirmed so much in church, and one Sunday she was mortified at something I did during the service. A woman in front of me had taken off her high-heeled slippers, so I got one of them between my toes and pulled it back underneath me. When the woman searched for her shoe with her bare foot, I began to giggle. Finally, I slid the shoe back under her pew, but Aunt Maggie saw me and pinched me so hard that I had a red spot on my behind.

After church we would return to the house for one of those unforgettable southern dinners—platters of fried chicken, cold country ham, fresh okra, corn on the cob, homemade hot rolls, and angel food cake with whipped cream and fresh peaches. Then I would slip out of the house in my Sunday clothes to explore the barn or the smokehouse. Sooner or later Aunt Maggie would corner me, sometimes on the highest limb of a peach or chinaberry tree, and I'd be shut in a bedroom to memorize the catechism.

One Sunday afternoon, I remember, my Sunday school class went out to a home for old folks. We had to go up on a stage one by one and recite a verse of the Bible, but I was so overcome by stage fright that I completely forgot the two words I was supposed to say: "Jesus wept."

A fourth great-aunt, Aunt Katie, lived across town and was married to Uncle Hector, the sheriff of Cumberland County. He never drove a car or carried a pistol, but truly he was my hero—a stately white-haired man who wore Teddy Roosevelt eyeglasses. When Aunt Katie discovered I didn't know my colors, she was determined to teach me. She'd got several boxes of crayons and would spread them out on the living-room floor, but it drove her into fits of exasperation that I could find the blue and yellow crayons with ease, but the browns, greens, and reds baffled me. She finally gave up and pronounced me color-blind.

Even today the stately Victorian house still stands, an immovable object that refuses to give way to the fine buildings that besiege it. It is a ghost of another time, soon to fall to progress. Our Negro cook, Maw-Maw, who changed my diapers more than once, is gone, and so are all the others except Aunt Eliza, now ninety years old. The white paint has peeled from the house, the plaster is breaking through the wallpaper, and the wooden latticework on the front porch, once like filigree of silver, is rotting away. But even today I could go out back to the smokehouse and dig up salt that dripped to the earth below where the hams had been hung to cure.

Times got better for my father, and his new wife came to get my sister and me from the three old ladies. All I can remember were some loud exchanges of words between my aunts and my father, then driving home in the black of night and screaming my head off when my father and new mother took me inside the Raeford home.

In the next four years I got three new sisters and a new brother. As soon as the youngest was able to walk, my father would pack the six of us in his old Dodge and take us to the Atlantic Ocean, about eighty miles away. I was always happiest when I got the first whiff of salt air. How my father afforded to give us this frequent excursion is still beyond me. I exulted in the majesty of the sea and was the most reluctant one in the family when the time came for us to go home.

It was on one of those trips, when I was eight or nine years old, that I decided I was going to become a photographer. Dad had an early Kodak fold-out camera, and he was pretty good with it. One morning when we were returning from the sea, he parked the Dodge at the end of a bridge overlooking the mouth of the Cape Fear River, where it dumped into the Atlantic, and aimed his camera down at a Navy destroyer docked below. When I saw the black-and-white print of the ship, which presented a ghostly image in the mist of the river, I never forgot what could be done with that black box.

Later, some bleak days came along for my father; my stepmother died when I was ten, and it was several years before he remarried—this time a school teacher who was, and still is, one of the guiding influences in my life. During those years, even though we had a caretaker, I was left to run free, always barefoot during the summer months, usually with skinned knees or healing scabs. That's when I began to reason out my own Creator in the taste of honeysuckle nectar, the meat of a hickory nut, wild blackberries, and hog apples. I would often camp out with a friend in those tall, wind-whispering North Carolina pines or drift down Rockfish Creek for miles on a raft we built of logs and planks. It's a wonder my father didn't turn gray overnight worrying about me.

I can remember summers and winter weekends when I worked on the farm of a boyhood friend three miles outside of town. I was eleven or twelve at the time. After we had done the chores—feeding the hogs and putting corn in the bins for the cattle—we'd play Monopoly or lie in our cold room and talk about what we were going to do when we grew up.

One of my most profound experiences arose because of a mule they gave me to plow furrows for tobacco planting. I was feeling pretty much alone that summer, as my stepmother had died the winter before, so the mule became my closest friend. It was just an ordinary mule, but it was very patient while I hitched it to the plow. Every morning before hitching it, I'd go to the corn crib, shuck an ear, and feed the animal. Pretty soon, it began to anticipate this little treat and would be waiting for me with its head over the pasture fence.

In the fall, when I returned to the farm for a weekend, I found my mule was gone. The next morning at breakfast I asked my friend's father what had happened to it. He gave me a big snort: "Durn you, boy, you ruined that mule! We couldn't get a lick of work out of it after you left." I never had the courage to ask the next obvious question—I suppose I knew that I had caused its death. It wasn't until years later that I unscrambled that unpleasant morning in my mind and exonerated myself of any blame. It was man's inhumanity all over again. Such a simple reward would have guaranteed that farmer the best mule on the place. Just a little act of kindness—an ear of corn to start the day.

As a boy, I always found work in July, when the watermelons were ripe. I would hang out at the train depot until a job turned up. At first my only employer was a sinewy Negro, who must have thought I was hungry because I looked so spindly in short pants. If you've never loaded boxcars with watermelons for five cents an hour, I can tell you it is an ordeal. Every couple of hours, though, the Negro would accidentally-on-purpose drop a melon—I got one half of the heart, he got the other, and the sparrows got the rinds. Soon I learned to pour some salt into my pocket before I went down to the depot.

After the watermelon season there were jobs in the cotton fields, picking at two cents a pound. I was a proud boy the first (and only) day I ever made two dollars. It was serious work. You got "chewed out" for leaving bits of cotton in the bolls, and if you skipped a row, you could get fired. Some of the fields were near the creek, and when the sun melted orange across the sky, the gunny sack was left in a heap beside a pair of short pants on the bank; the little whirlpools of dark water were the balm that salved aching limbs and parched feet, and made you sleep like a stone.

Even in those days, I felt a yearning to express a cloud as white as the cotton, towering acres high into the sky, or to take a picture of the field, patchworked with the bent figures toiling there, or to remember the Negroes' shacks, black against the crimson sky. No, you don't have to travel far in search of beauty. It is at every turn of the road, in every leaf that crisps under your naked feet. It is in the call of a locust embedded in the tall, frightening pines, and in the start you get when a lizard fleets across your path; it is in the dark curdling pools of the creek, iridescent in the evening light; in the smell of a pine cone or the call of the whippoorwill. It is when you make yourself dizzy as you walk along a familiar path at night looking up at a starry sky, somehow knowing that among all those millions of lights, you also are being observed from afar.

Later, during my teens when my interest in photography began to materialize, I'm sure I nearly drove my parents crazy. My high school principal took me under his wing and taught me to develop and print pictures. Then I decided I could turn my hobby into a financial success, so I began to process pictures for my friends. I cleaned out the closet in my bedroom and devised a lab just big enough to turn around in. There was only one problem—my closet was above the living room, and I continually sloshed chemicals out of the trays. They dripped right down the living-room wall and left permanent brown stains. Needless to say, I was given an ultimatum. When I took this problem of no lab to the principal, he organized a photography club and found us space in the chemistry department for a lab.

Because I grew up with them, old things fascinate me: the ice cream churn, the apple peeler, the beautiful marbled pots and pans. I sometimes wonder about the faces and personalities of the people who owned these treasures that I collect today for still lifes. What has become of them? Is this all there is left to show for a human life? I am driven to do studies of these things, these memories that come whispering back to life from out of my past.

I love to browse through antique shops, sniffing the musty air and hunting for the discarded relic that the dealer will sell for a buck when it is worth a fortune to me because of its exquisite shape or coloring, the scrapes, dents, and rusty spots that only time can bestow.

Sometimes I buy an old pitcher, lantern, pot, or other kitchen item and it stays around the studio for months before I go back to it. For example, I've had a stereoscope for a year, tried a couple of studies with it, but tossed them out. I just haven't let that particular subject ferment in my mind long enough to place it in the right setting. It's almost as if I have to move through time and engage the freshness of that memory. Then all the pieces fall into place. When I feel real excitement at seeing the finished work, I know that it is right.

I can't create on demand. Often people will bring me something old to use in a study, but their generosity is more often than not the kiss of death. If it isn't an object I discovered for myself, knowing instantly that it had the ingredients for which I was searching, I'll probably never use it. When I place it before the camera, I must be able to see it for the beauty of its form or texture, letting recollections of my first response to it come flickering back into consciousness.

Many people comment that my work is sad and haunting. Others say it is steeped in religious overtones, though I don't see it that way. I would call myself a chronicler of my own memories and experiences. But it goes even deeper than that. What you see on the surface may be only an onion or cattails shedding their "parachutes," but what I really want you to see is the divine plan behind it all. Perhaps you didn't make ice cream in an old churn, or have a creek an hour's walk away. Maybe you see nothing in the way the wind plants new dandelion seeds, or in the thought it took to invent such a plan for sowing. I yearn for you to refresh your own perspective on the beauty of the world, to look at the whole apple before you bite into it. I want you to acknowledge that each of us is endowed with the gift of life and that, for all its brevity and pain, it is truly a gift.

Twenty years ago, a photographer couldn't get his foot in the door of an art gallery, much less hang his work. But twenty years ago a woman bought twenty Brillo boxes for $500 each and called them art because she'd bought them from a gallery. Twenty years ago a canvas painted solid black took the $1,000 first prize in an art contest. Twenty years ago you could buy an American cut-glass punch bowl for $25 (today it's worth $2,500). Memories and heritage are being rediscovered. People everywhere realize that something rare and dear to them is being lost forever, and they want to reclaim some wisp of those precious years, soon to be obliterated. Simplicity, too, we crave —the beauty of a sunset, still beautiful beyond the clutter we have spread over this natural garden that we occupy. Somehow, it is the duty of the poet, the artist, the musician to preserve for us the remaining fragments of the lives of our pioneer ancestors and to recall and reshape this legacy for our computer-age senses.

Sometime you may find an old apple peeler like the one in my photograph. When you study its gears and cogs, and finally watch it peel an apple, the machine will dazzle your brain. Or how about the sewing machine? It wasn't invented yesterday. There were some smart boys back in those days, who made everybody's life a little easier with their inventions.

One cannot paint the sound of a train moaning in the night or rain whispering on autumn leaves, the pungent odor of sugarcane being squeezed into syrup, the glimmer of fireflies in the night, or the awesome trail of a falling star. The artist, in his own individual way, is a town crier proclaiming that beauty is everywhere and that we of all creatures are endowed with thought, memory, speech, and love to understand this earth.

So many times people have said to me, "I wish I had a talent." I learned a great lesson once from a stranger beside me at a party. Our host, a gifted pianist, was playing one of Beethoven's sonatas. I whispered to the stranger, "I'd give anything to be able to do that." He glared and replied, "What's the matter with you? God gave you a talent." And so he did, to each of us. Which is the more worthy, the artist or he who benefits from the art? They are equals. Understanding a friend with problems can also be an art; so can nursing the aged, or just appreciating everyday living. Art takes all forms and guises. If I did not believe it exists in all of us, I would have exposed my last strip of film long ago.

Down by the Barn

THE BARN LOFT

WEATHERED BEAMS

PUSSY WILLOWS

LOVE LETTERS

THE POTTING SHED

CRATING EGGS

THE SURREY

AUTUMN LEAVES

MOLLIE'S SPRINKLER

YESTERDAY'S DREAM

HONEYSUCKLE

BROWN COUNTY

THE MILKING STOOL

Grandma's Kitchen

FRESHLY LAID

MAKIN' CORN STICKS

THE BUTTER MOLD

BREAD N' HONEY

THE PEARL

BLUE CHEESE

CATTAILS

IRON POTS

KEEPIN' WARM

On a Hot Afternoon

STRAWBERRY ICE CREAM

THE BALL OF YARN

MINUET

AFTER THE WASH

SEWING BASKET

FIRST PEEP

PEGGY'S PLAYMATES

LEMONADE

Harvest Time

CONCORD GRAPES

ALMOST RIPE

BLUEBERRIES

THE ORCHARD GATE

CIDER TIME

BUSHEL O' GOLD

WASHIN' CHERRIES

THE PANTRY

Goin' home

SCHOOL'S OUT

ANGLE OF REPOSE

THE GILDED CAGE

THE OLD STONE BRIDGE

IVIED WALLS

RESURRECTION

FRANK'S CORNFIELD

THE HOMESTEAD

WINDY HILL